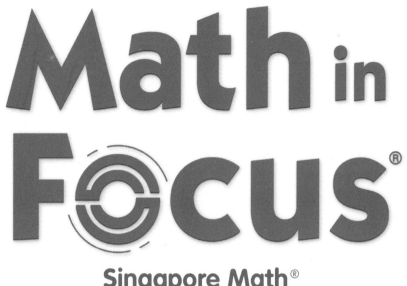

Math in Focus®

Singapore Math®
by Marshall Cavendish

Extra Practice
and Homework

Program Consultant
Dr. Fong Ho Kheong

U.S. Distributor

 Marshall Cavendish Education

 Houghton Mifflin Harcourt.
The Learning Company™

Course **2B**

© 2020 Marshall Cavendish Education Pte Ltd

Published by Marshall Cavendish Education
Times Centre, 1 New Industrial Road, Singapore 536196
Customer Service Hotline: (65) 6213 9688
US Office Tel: (1-914) 332 8888 | Fax: (1-914) 332 8882
E-mail: cs@mceducation.com
Website: www.mceducation.com

Distributed by
Houghton Mifflin Harcourt
125 High Street
Boston, MA 02110
Tel: 617-351-5000
Website: www.hmhco.com/programs/math-in-focus

First published 2020

ISBN 978-0-358-10311-0

Printed in Singapore

3 4 5 6 7 8 9 10   1401   26 25 24 23 22
4500840182   B C D E F

The cover image shows a Eurasian lynx.
This medium-sized wild cat can be found in the thick forests of Siberia, and in remote, mountainous parts of Europe and Asia. Eurasian lynxes have dark spots on their fur, long, black tufts at the tips of their ears, and they have excellent hearing. They are nocturnal hunters that approach their unsuspecting prey very quietly from out of the darkness. Although their numbers had previously dropped due to hunting, they are now increasing once again.

Contents

Chapter 9   **Probability of Compound Events**

Preface

Welcome!

Math in Focus®: *Extra Practice and Homework* is written to complement the Student Edition in your learning journey.

The book provides carefully constructed activities and problems that parallel what you have learned in the Student Edition.

- **Activities** are designed to help you achieve proficiency in the math concepts and to develop confidence in your mathematical abilities.

- **MATH JOURNAL** is included to provide you with opportunities to reflect on the learning in the chapter.

- **PUT ON YOUR THINKING CAP!** allows you to improve your critical thinking and problem-solving skills, as well as to be challenged as you solve problems in novel ways.

You may use a calculator whenever ▦ appears.

BLANK

Chapter 5

Extra Practice and Homework
Angle Properties and Straight Lines

Activity 1 Complementary, Supplementary, and Adjacent Angles

State whether each pair of angles is complementary.

1 m∠A = 76° and m∠B = 14°

2 m∠C = 10° and m∠D = 80°

3 m∠E = 37° and m∠F = 63°

4 m∠G = 76° and m∠H = 4°

State whether each pair of angles is supplementary.

5 m∠A = 79° and m∠B = 11°

6 m∠C = 96° and m∠D = 111°

7 m∠E = 146° and m∠F = 34°

8 m∠G = 81° and m∠H = 99°

Find the measure of the complement of the angle with the given measure.

9 20°

10 41°

11 9°

12 73°

Find the measure of the supplement of the angle with the given measure.

13 13°

14 97°

15 109°

16 168°

© 2020 Marshall Cavendish Education Pte Ltd

The diagrams may not be drawn to scale. ∠ABD and ∠DBC are complementary angles. Find the value of x.

17

18

The diagrams may not be drawn to scale. ∠PQS and ∠SQR are supplementary angles. Find the value of m.

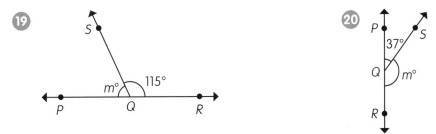

19

20

Find the measures of the complement and the supplement of each given angle measure, where possible.

21 m∠Y = 83°

22 m∠Z = 71°

Identify all the angles in each diagram. State which angles are adjacent.

The diagrams may not be drawn to scale. The measure of ∠PQR is 90°. Find the value of x.

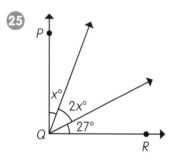

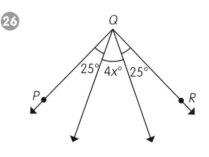

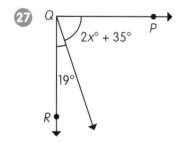

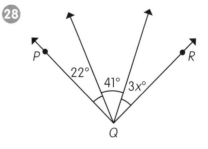

The diagrams may not be drawn to scale. $\overleftrightarrow{PR}$ is a straight line. Find the value of *m*.

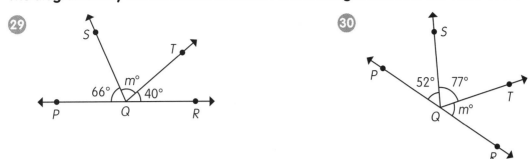

29

30

The diagrams may not be drawn to scale. In each diagram, the ratio of *a* to *b* = 1 : 4. Find the values of *a* and *b*.

31 The measure of $\angle PQR = 90°$

32 $\overleftrightarrow{PR}$ is a straight line

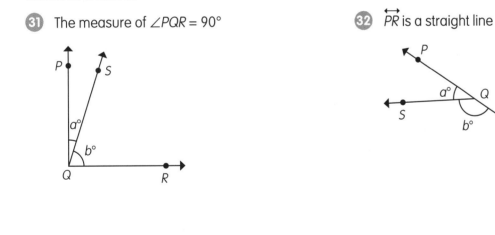

Solve.

33 The measures of two complementary angles are in the ratio of 2 : 7. Find the measures of the two angles.

You can use the four-step problem-solving model to help you.

34 The diagram shows a gate. $\overleftrightarrow{AC}$ and $\overrightarrow{BE}$ are perpendicular to each other. Jordan says that $\angle ABD$, $\angle DBF$, and $\angle CBF$ are supplementary angles. Do you agree? Explain your answer.

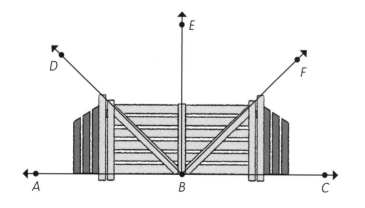

Recall the definition of supplementary angles.

Activity 2 Angles that Share a Vertex

The diagrams may not be drawn to scale. Find the value of each variable *x*.

1

150°

x°

2

92°
46°
x°
137°

3

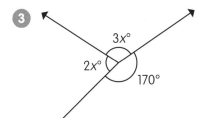

3*x*°
2*x*°
170°

4

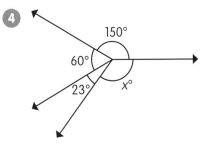

150°
60°
23°
x°

5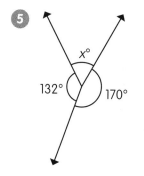

$x°$

$132°$ $170°$

6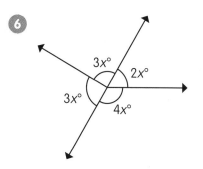

$3x°$ $2x°$

$3x°$

$4x°$

7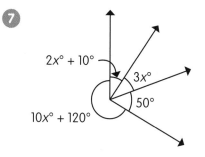

$2x° + 10°$

$3x°$

$50°$

$10x° + 120°$

8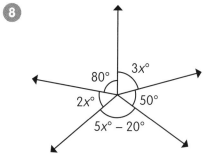

$80°$ $3x°$

$2x°$ $50°$

$5x° − 20°$

Name the pairs of vertical angles.

9 $\overleftrightarrow{AB}$ and $\overleftrightarrow{CD}$ are straight lines.

10 $\overleftrightarrow{PQ}$ and $\overleftrightarrow{RS}$ are straight lines.

11 $\overleftrightarrow{AC}$ and $\overleftrightarrow{ED}$ are straight lines.

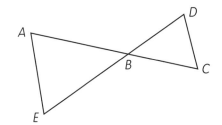

12 $\overleftrightarrow{AD}$ and $\overleftrightarrow{FC}$ are straight lines.

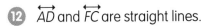
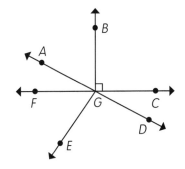

13 $\overleftrightarrow{AB}$, $\overleftrightarrow{CD}$, and $\overleftrightarrow{EF}$ are straight lines.

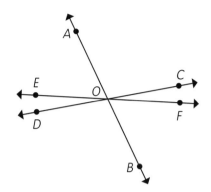

14 $\overleftrightarrow{AB}$ and $\overleftrightarrow{CD}$ are straight lines.

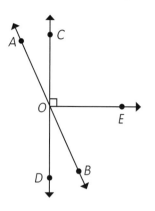

The diagrams may not be drawn to scale. Find the value of each variable.

15 $\overleftrightarrow{AB}$ and $\overleftrightarrow{CD}$ are straight lines.

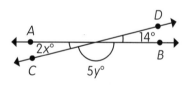

16 $\overleftrightarrow{AB}$, $\overleftrightarrow{CD}$, and $\overleftrightarrow{EF}$ are straight lines.

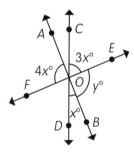

17 $\overleftrightarrow{AB}$ is a straight line.

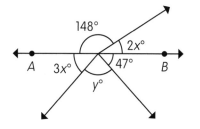

18 $\overleftrightarrow{AB}$ and $\overleftrightarrow{CD}$ are straight lines.

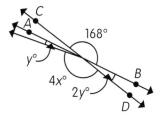

Solve.

19 If $\angle A$ and $\angle B$ are angles at a point and m$\angle A$ = 133°, what is m$\angle B$?

20 If 108°, 34°, 91°, and $p°$ are angles at a point, what is the value of p?

21 In the diagram, p, q, r, and s are in the ratio $3 : 2 : 1 : 4$. Find the value of each variable.

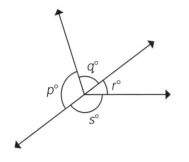

22 The diagram shows the flag of Jamaica. Name the pairs of vertical angles.

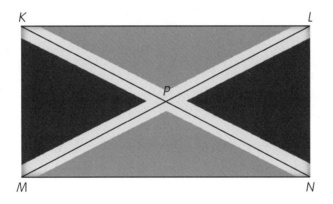

Activity 3 Alternate Interior, Alternate Exterior, and Corresponding Angles

$\overleftrightarrow{PQ}$ and $\overleftrightarrow{RS}$ are parallel lines. $\overleftrightarrow{TU}$ is a straight line. Identify each pair of angles as vertical, corresponding, alternate interior, alternate exterior angles, or none of the above.

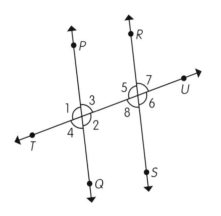

1 ∠1 and ∠5

2 ∠3 and ∠8

3 ∠4 and ∠7

4 ∠5 and ∠6

5 Name all angles that have the same measure as ∠2.

$\overleftrightarrow{MN}$ is parallel to $\overleftrightarrow{PQ}$. $\overleftrightarrow{ST}$ is a straight line. Use the diagram to answer each question.

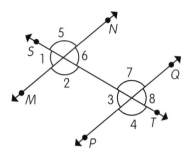

6 Name all angles that have the same measure as ∠7.

7 If m∠1 = 30°, find m∠8.

8 If m∠2 = 140°, find m∠3.

The diagrams may not be drawn to scale. Find the measure of each numbered angle.

9 $\overleftrightarrow{AB}$ is parallel to $\overleftrightarrow{CD}$.

10 $\overrightarrow{BA}$ is parallel to $\overrightarrow{DC}$.

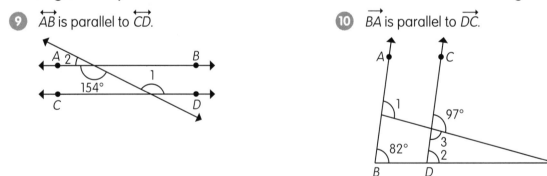

11 $\overleftrightarrow{AB}$ is parallel to $\overleftrightarrow{CD}$.

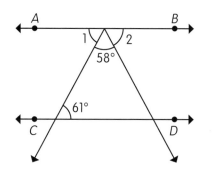

12 $\overrightarrow{BA}$ is parallel to $\overrightarrow{DC}$.

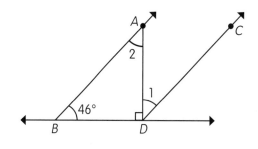

13 $\overleftrightarrow{AB}$ is parallel to $\overleftrightarrow{CD}$.

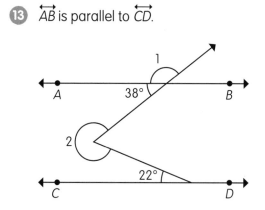

14 $\overleftrightarrow{AB}$ is parallel to $\overleftrightarrow{CD}$.

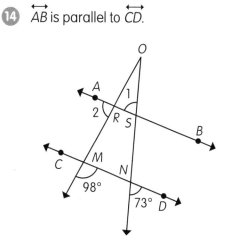

The diagrams may not be drawn to scale. $\overleftrightarrow{AB}$ is parallel to $\overleftrightarrow{CD}$. Find the value of each variable.

15

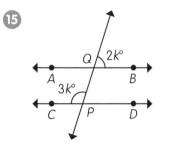

16

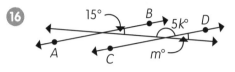

17

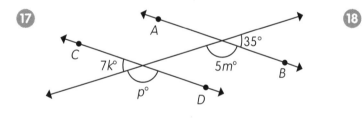

18

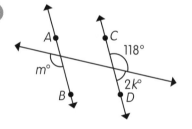

The diagrams may not be drawn to scale. $\overleftrightarrow{AB}$ is parallel to $\overleftrightarrow{CD}$ and $\overleftrightarrow{MN}$ is parallel to $\overleftrightarrow{PQ}$. Find the measure of each numbered angle.

19

20

21

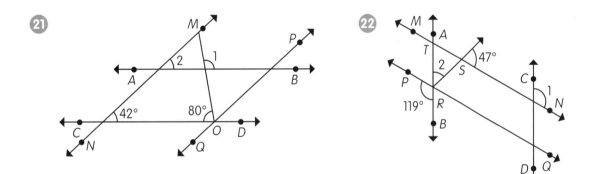

22

The diagrams may not be drawn to scale. Find the value of each variable.

23 $\overrightarrow{BA}$ is parallel to $\overrightarrow{DE}$.

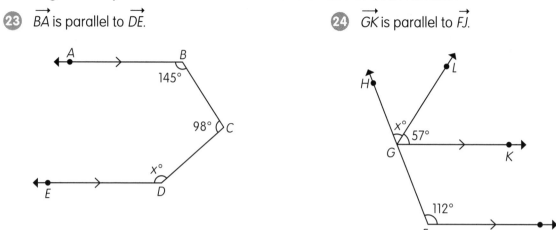

24 $\overrightarrow{GK}$ is parallel to $\overrightarrow{FJ}$.

25 $\overrightarrow{MP}$ is parallel to $\overrightarrow{NR}$.

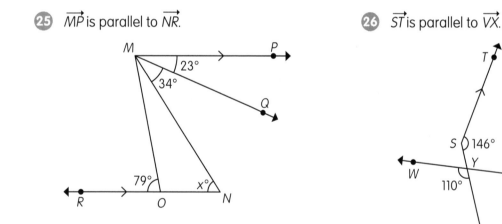

26 $\overrightarrow{ST}$ is parallel to $\overrightarrow{VX}$.

© 2020 Marshall Cavendish Education Pte Ltd

Solve.

27 The diagram below shows the flag of the Czech Republic. $\overleftrightarrow{MN}$, $\overleftrightarrow{PQ}$, and $\overleftrightarrow{RS}$ are parallel lines. $\overleftrightarrow{AB}$ and $\overleftrightarrow{CD}$ are straight lines.

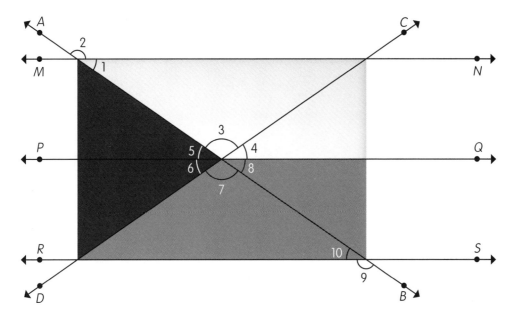

a Name two alternate exterior angles.

b Name all angles that have the same measure as $\angle 10$.

28 In the diagram below, $\overleftrightarrow{AB}$ is parallel to $\overleftrightarrow{CD}$ and $\overleftrightarrow{PQ}$ is a straight line. Given that $m\angle 1 = (20k + 18)°$ and $m\angle 2 = 78°$, find the value of k.

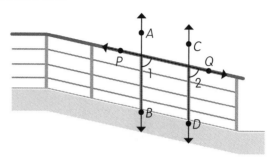

Chapter 5

Extra Practice and Homework
Angle Properties and Straight Lines

Activity 4   Interior and Exterior Angles

The diagrams may not be drawn to scale. Find the value of *x*.

1 *ABC* is an isosceles triangle.

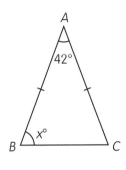

2

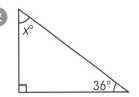

3 $\overline{AD}$ and $\overline{BC}$ are straight lines.

4 $\overrightarrow{QS}$ is a straight line.

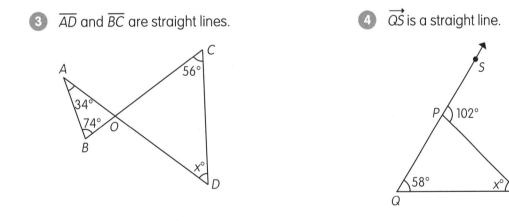

The diagrams may not be drawn to scale. Find the measure of each numbered angle.

5

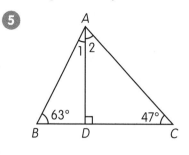

6 $AB = AC = DC$

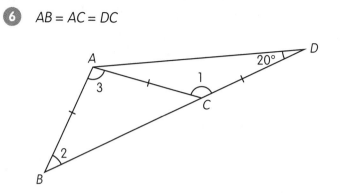

7

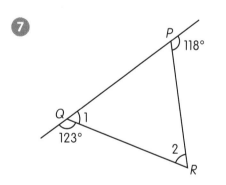

8

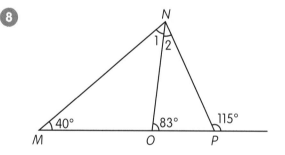

Extra Practice and Homework Course 2B

The diagrams may not be drawn to scale. $\overline{AB}$ is parallel to $\overline{CD}$. Find the value of y.

9

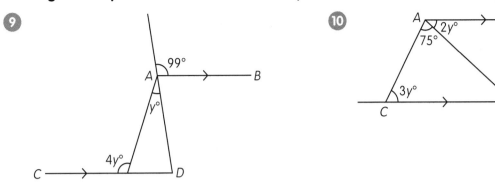

10

11

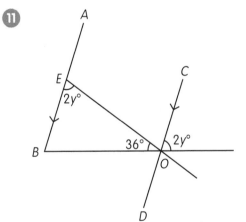

12

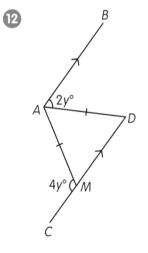

Find the value of *x* and name each triangle.

13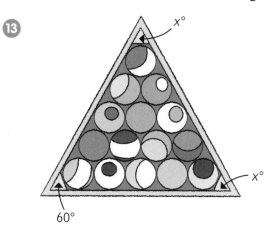

14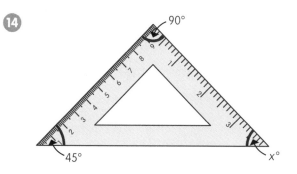

15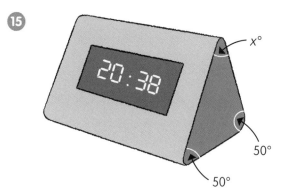

16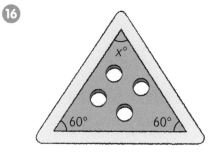

© 2020 Marshall Cavendish Education Pte Ltd

The diagrams may not be drawn to scale. $\overline{AB}$ **is parallel to** $\overline{CD}$**. Find the measure of each numbered angle.**

17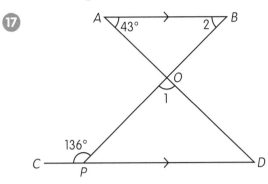

18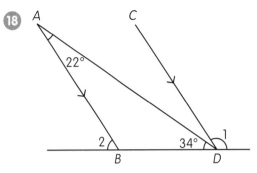

19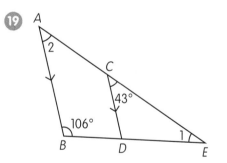

20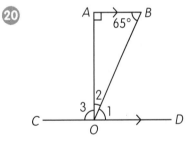

Solve.

21 $m\angle 1 = m\angle 2 = (5x - 10)°$ and $m\angle 3 = (2x + 8)°$. Use an equation to find the value of x and then find the measures of $\angle 1$, $\angle 2$, and $\angle 3$.

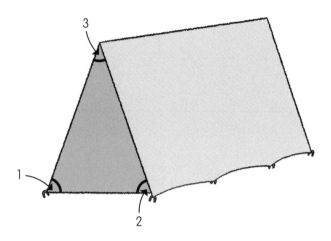

22 $\overline{PQ}$ is parallel to $\overline{RS}$. Given that $m\angle 1 = 60°$ and $m\angle 2 = 120°$, find the measures of $\angle 3$ and $\angle 4$.

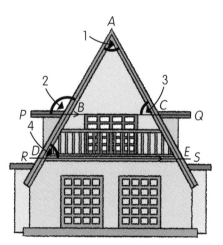

Name: _____   Date: _____

Mathematical Habit 3 Construct viable arguments

Jake has answered the question below incorrectly.

In the diagram, $\overleftrightarrow{AB}$ is parallel to $\overleftrightarrow{DC}$ and $\overline{AD}$ is parallel to line $\overline{BC}$. Find the values of p, q, and r.

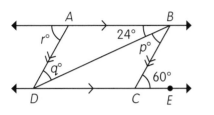

Jake's answer:

$m\angle p = 90° - 24°$ (Comp. $\angle$s)
$\quad = 66°$

$m\angle q = 66°$ (Alt. int. $\angle$s)

$m\angle r = 66° + 24°$ (Ext. $\angle$ of triangle)
$\quad\quad = 90°$

Explain to Jake his mistake by identifying the specific step in which the error occurred and show him the correct solution.

Solve.

1 | **Mathematical Habit** | **2** | Use mathematical reasoning

In the diagram, $\overline{AD}$ is parallel to $\overline{BE}$ and $\overline{BD}$ is parallel to $\overline{CE}$. Find the values of k, n, and p.

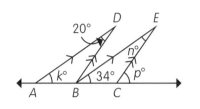

2 | **Mathematical Habit** | **2** | Use mathematical reasoning

In the diagram, $\overleftrightarrow{PR}$ is parallel to $\overleftrightarrow{SU}$. Find the value of f.

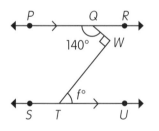

Chapter 6

Extra Practice and Homework
Geometric Construction

Activity 1 Constructing Triangles

Use the given information to construct each triangle.

1 Triangle *PQR*, where *PQ* = 6 cm, *QR* = 7 cm, and m∠*PQR* = 80°.

2 Triangle *ABC*, where *AB* = 7 cm, m∠*ABC* = 115°, and m∠*BAC* = 25°.

Triangle *XYZ*, where *XY* = 4.6 cm, *YZ* = 5.4 cm, and *XZ* = 8 cm.

4 Triangle *KLM*, where *KL* = 8 cm, *LM* = 6 cm, and *KM* = 10 cm.

5 Triangle *DEF*, where *DE* = 9 cm, m∠*EDF* = 30°, and m∠*DEF* = 50°.

6 Triangle *STU*, where *ST* = 8.4 cm, *TU* = 6 cm, and m∠*STU* = 65°.

Solve.

7 Construct a triangle *XYZ* in which *XY* = 4 cm, *YZ* = 3 cm, and m∠*XYZ* = 90°.

    a Determine the number of triangles that can be constructed.

    b Find the possible length(s) of *XZ*.

8 Construct triangle *ABC* in which *AB* = 7 cm, *AC* = 4.8 cm, and m∠*ABC* = 40°. Is there more than one triangle that you can draw with these dimensions? If so, what are all the possible measures of ∠*BAC*?

Chapter 6

Extra Practice and Homework
Geometric Construction

Activity 2 Scale Drawings and Lengths

Solve.

1. Roy built a model of a ferris wheel. The model has a height of 18 inches. The actual ferris wheel has a height of 234 feet. What scale factor did Roy use for the model?

On a blueprint, the height of a door is 3.5 inches. The actual height of the door is 7 feet. What is the scale on the blueprint?

3 A model of space shuttle Apollo Saturn V is created with a scale of 1 : 144. The actual space shuttle has a width of 62.4 feet. What is the width of the model, in inches?

Tim has a model of an armoured vehicle created using a scale of 1 : 72. The length of the model is 3.3 inches. What is the actual length of the vehicle, in feet?

5 A road map uses a scale of 1 inch : 4 miles. The distance on the map between two towns is 3.8 inches. What is the actual distance between these two towns?

A map shows some cities in the northern part of the United States. The scale of the map is 1 inch : 125 miles.

a The actual distance between Chicago, IL and Pittsburgh, PA is 375 miles. Find the distance between the two cities on the map.

b On the map, the distance between Washington, D.C., and New York City is 1.5 inches. Find the actual distance between these two cities.

7 Maria drew a picture of a flower and then made a reduced photocopy of her drawing. The flower in the actual drawing is 6 inches long. The flower in the reduced copy is 4.5 inches long. Find the scale factor of the reduction.

8 The Truckee River is about 142 miles long. What is the length of this river on a map with a scale of 1 inch : 25 miles?

The scale of a map is 1 inch : 5 miles. The length of Manila Creek Road on this map is 3.4 inches. Find the actual length of the road.

10 The length of a field on a scale drawing is 3.5 inches. The scale on the drawing is 1 inch : 9 feet. The field is redrawn using a new scale of 1 inch : 3 feet. What will be the length of the redrawn field?

11 The diagrams show triangle *XYZ* in which *XY* = 6 cm and *YZ* = 8 cm, and its reduction, triangle *PQR* in which *QR* = 4 cm.

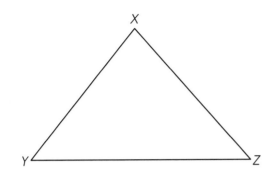 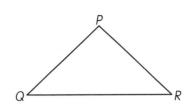

a Find the scale factor of the reduction.

b Find the length of *PQ*.

12 Explain what is scale factor greater than one and what is scale factor less than one. Illustrate with examples.

The size of the image remains unchanged when the scale factor is 1.

Chapter

6

Extra Practice and Homework
Geometric Construction

Activity 3   Scale Drawings and Areas

Solve.

1 The scale on a blueprint is 1 inch : 9 feet.

a The area of the basketball court is 58 square inches. What is the actual area of the basketball court?

b The length of the basketball court on the blueprint is 10.4 inches. What is the actual length of the basketball court?

c What is the actual width of the basketball court to the nearest foot?

2 Use the scale on the dormitory floor plan to find each of the following measures.

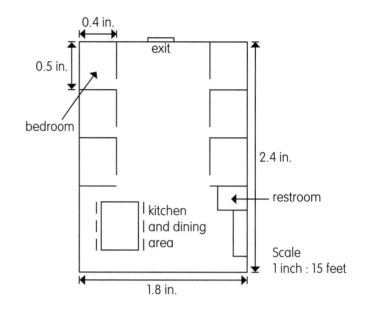

a The actual length and width of a bedroom

b The actual width of the exit door is 4.5 feet. What is the width of this door on the floor plan?

c The actual floor area of the whole dormitory

Mathematical Habit 3 Construct viable arguments

Ben has answered the question below incorrectly.

A plan of a school is drawn using a scale of 1 cm : 3 m. The drawn school canteen measures 4 cm by 4 cm on the plan. Calculate the actual area of the canteen, in square meters.

Ben's working
Scale of plan is 1 : 3.
This means that the actual school canteen is 3 times of the canteen drawn on the plan.
Area of canteen on plan = 4 · 4
$\qquad$ = 16 cm²
Actual area = 16 · 3
$\qquad$ = 48 m²

Find Ben's mistakes and explain by showing the correct solution.

Mathematical Habit 2 Use mathematical reasoning

With the given information below, classify which are the information that will allow you to construct a unique triangle.

> three sides
>
> two angles and the side between the angles
>
> two sides and the angle that is between the sides
>
> three angles
>
> one side and three angles

Information that is Needed to Construct a Unique Triangle	Information that is Not Enough to Construct a Unique Triangle

Chapter 7

Extra Practice and Homework
Circumference, Area, Volume, and Surface Area

Activity 1   Radius, Diameter, and Circumference of a Circle

O is the center of the circle and $\overline{AB}$ is a straight line. Fill in each blank.

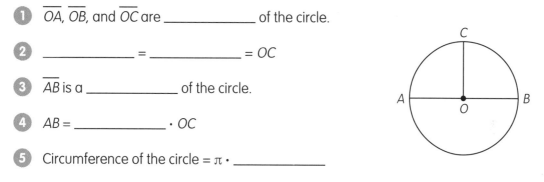

1 $\overline{OA}$, $\overline{OB}$, and $\overline{OC}$ are _____ of the circle.

2 _____ = _____ = OC

3 $\overline{AB}$ is a _____ of the circle.

4 AB = _____ · OC

5 Circumference of the circle = π · _____

Find the circumference of each circle. Use $\frac{22}{7}$ as an approximation for π.

6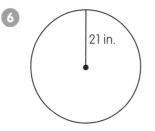
21 in.

7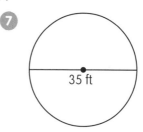
35 ft

8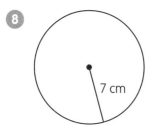
7 cm

9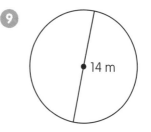
14 m

Find the length of each arc. Use $\frac{22}{7}$ as an approximation for π.

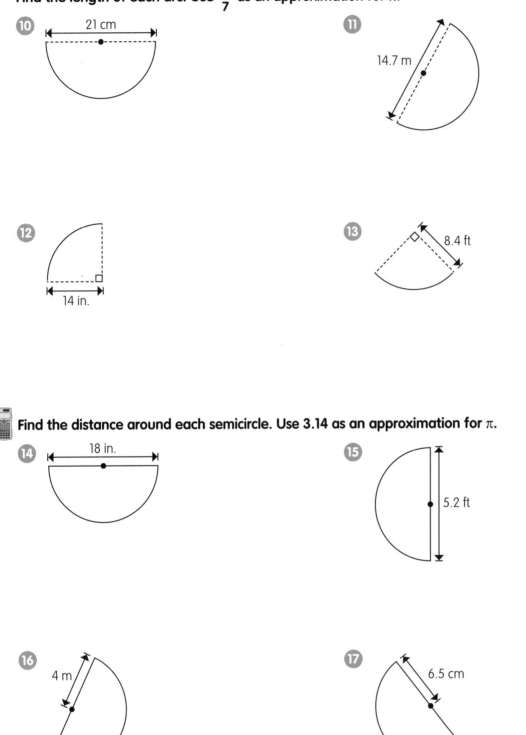

10 21 cm

11 14.7 m

12 14 in.

13 8.4 ft

Find the distance around each semicircle. Use 3.14 as an approximation for π.

14 18 in.

15 5.2 ft

16 4 m

17 6.5 cm

Find the distance around each quadrant. Use $\frac{22}{7}$ as an approximation for π.

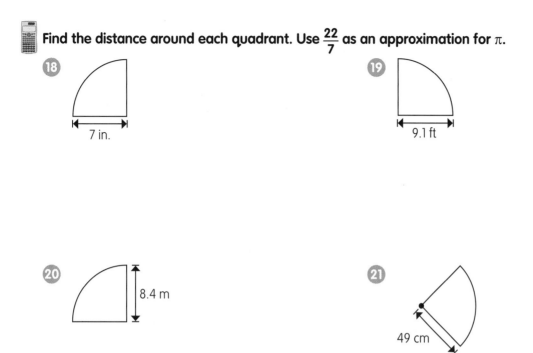

⑱

7 in.

⑲

9.1 ft

⑳

8.4 m

㉑

49 cm

Solve. Use 3.14 as an approximation for π.

㉒ The radius of a circle is 10 feet. Find its circumference.

23 The diameter of a semicircle is 8 centimeters. Find its distance around the semicircle.

24 The radius of the wheel is 1.2 feet. What is the distance traveled when the wheel turns 20 times?

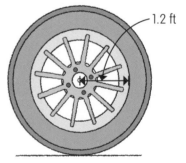

1.2 ft

Chapter

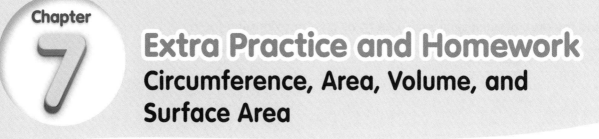

7

Extra Practice and Homework
Circumference, Area, Volume, and Surface Area

Activity 2   Area of a Circle

Find the area of each circle. Use 3.14 as an approximation for π.

1

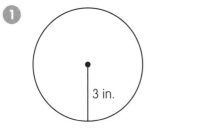

3 in.

2

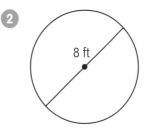

8 ft

Find the area of each circle. Use $\frac{22}{7}$ as an approximation for π.

3

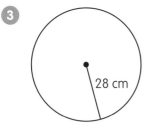

28 cm

4

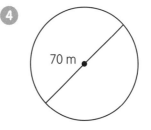

70 m

Find the area of each semicircle. Use $\frac{22}{7}$ as an approximation for π.

5 35 cm

6 84 in.

Find the area of each quarter circle. Use $\frac{22}{7}$ as an approximation for π.

7 14 m

8 21 ft

Solve. Use 3.14 as an approximation for π.

9   The diameter of a semicircle is 8 inches. Find its area.

10   The radius of a quarter circle is 12 centimeters. Find its area.

11 The shape of a cake is a circle. It is cut into 4 equal pieces.

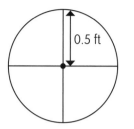

0.5 ft

a Find the area of the cake.

b Find the area of each of the 4 equal pieces.

Extra Practice and Homework
Circumference, Area, Volume, and Surface Area

Activity 3 Real-World Problems: Circles

Solve. Use 3.14 as an approximation for π.

1. Ivan and his friends shared a piece of circular waffle. Ivan has a quarter of a waffle. The radius of the waffle is 3.5 inches. What is the circumference of the whole waffle?

3.5 in.

2 The diameter of a semicircular pond is 3 meters. A squirrel moves around the pond twice. What is the distance covered by the squirrel?

3 The diameter of the pouch is 6 inches. Find the area of one semicircular side of the pouch.

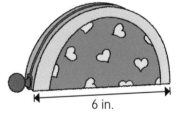

6 in.

4 Two pizzas were cut into quarters each. The radius of each quarter piece is 14 centimeters. Peter ate 3 quarters of the pizzas. Find the area of the remaining pizzas.

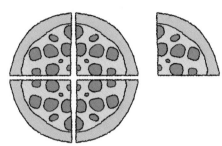

5 Jeff bent a wire into the shape of a quarter circle. The radius of the quarter circle is 3 inches. Find the length of the wire.

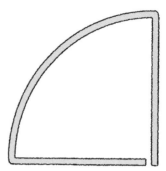

6 The diameter of a hula hoop is 3.2 feet. Find the circumference of the hula hoop.

7 The diameter of a semicircular fan is 24 centimeters. Find the area of the fan.

8   The picture shows a semicircular table. The outer diameter of the table is 11 feet and the width of the table top is 2 feet. What is the area of the table top?

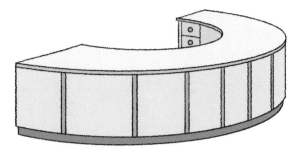

Draw a diagram to help you find the inner diameter of the table.

Chapter 7 — Extra Practice and Homework
Circumference, Area, Volume, and Surface Area

Activity 4   Area of Composite Figures

Find the area of each composite figure.

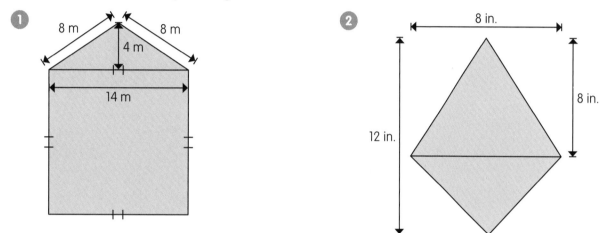

1   8 m   8 m   4 m   14 m

2   8 in.   8 in.   12 in.

Find the area of each shaded region. Use 3.14 as an approximation for π.

3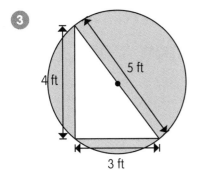

4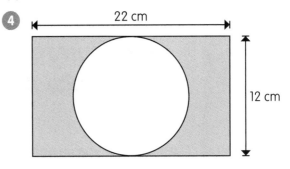

Solve.

5 The figure below is made up of a square and a right triangle. Find the area of the figure.

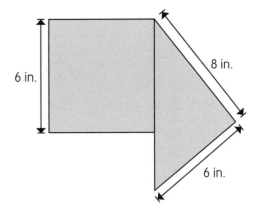

6 The figure below is made up of a triangle and a rectangle. Find the area of the figure.

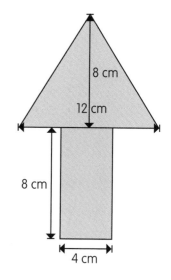

7 Jack creates a pencil shape using a semicircle, a rectangle, and a triangle. Find the total area of the shape. Use 3.14 as an approximation for π.

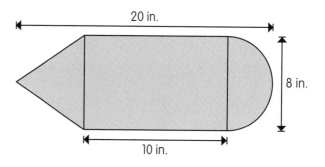

8 Find the area of the shaded region. Use 3.14 as an approximation for π.

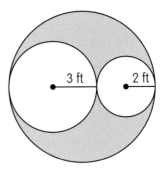

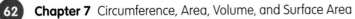

Chapter

7

Extra Practice and Homework
Circumference, Area, Volume, and Surface Area

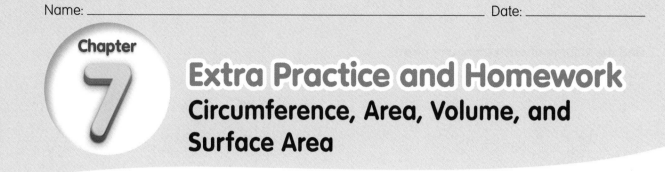

Activity 5   Volume of Prisms

State whether slices parallel to each given slice will form uniform cross sections.
If not, explain why.

1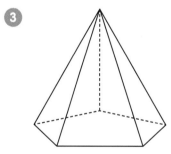

2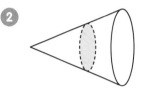

Each solid is sliced twice parallel to its base. Draw the two cross sections.

3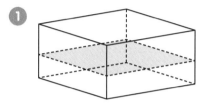

4

Find the volume of each triangular prism.

5

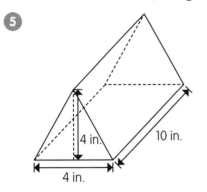

4 in.

10 in.

4 in.

6

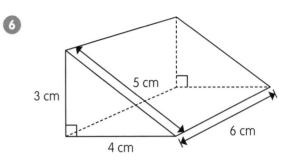

3 cm

5 cm

4 cm

6 cm

Solve.

7 The volume of the cuboid is 360 cubic feet. Find the height of the cuboid.

? ft

3 ft

12 ft

8 The base of the figure is a trapezoid. Find the volume of the prism.

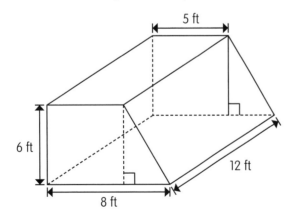

5 ft

6 ft

12 ft

8 ft

Chapter 7

Extra Practice and Homework
Circumference, Area, Volume, and Surface Area

Activity 6 Real-World Problems: Surface Area and Volume

Solve.

1. Jacob built a solid block using cubes of sides 3 centimeters as shown. He painted the surface area of the solid block. Find the surface area of the solid block.

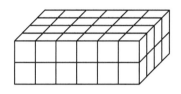

> Find the number of squares on each of the six sides of the solid block. Note that the opposite sides have the same number of squares.

2 A block of chocolate has measurements as shown.

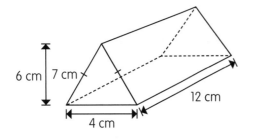

a What is the volume of the block of chocolate?

b It is wrapped using a piece of aluminum foil. What is the area of the aluminum foil used?

3 The diagram shows a loaf of bread, which is in the shape of a prism. The base of the prism is made up of a semicircle and a rectangle. Find the volume of the bread. Use 3.14 as an approximation for π.

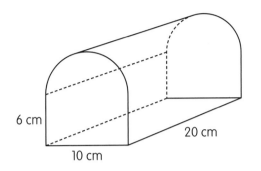

6 cm

20 cm

10 cm

4 A thermal mug in the shape of a cylinder, with radius 3.5 centimeters, has a capacity of 385 cubic centimeters. What is the height of the mug? Use $\frac{22}{7}$ as an approximation for π.

Mathematical Habit 2 Use mathematical reasoning

Jeff thinks that he can fill the 4-foot cubical tank with two 2-foot cubical tanks of water. Is he correct? Explain.

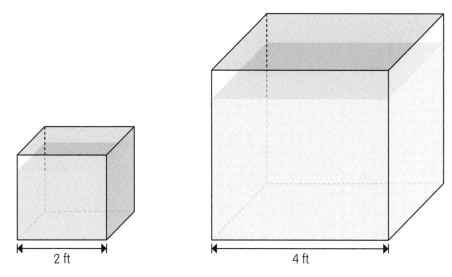

2 ft

4 ft

Mathematical Habit **1** Persevere in solving problems

The diagram shows a tent and the area of the canvas is made up of 4 trapezoids, and 4 rectangles. Calculate the area of canvas needed to make the tent shown.

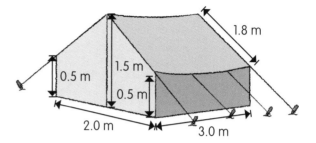

Chapter 8

Extra Practice and Homework
Statistics and Probability

Activity 1   Random Sampling Methods

State which sampling method or methods are being described for ① to ③.

① To determine the average number of hours people spend per day surfing the Internet, a researcher divided the population into groups according to age. Then, he randomly selected 100 people from each age group.

② As oranges are unloaded from a truck, Juan picks every 20th orange until he has collected 50 oranges to estimate the average mass of the oranges.

③ To study the level of water pollution of a river, water samples were taken from 50 locations along the course of the river.

Refer to the situation below to answer 4 to 6.

A survey was conducted to find the average height of middle school students. The height of 900 sixth-grade, seventh-grade, and eighth-grade students were recorded.

4　Explain the possible reasons why a simple random sampling method is not suitable.

5　Describe how a systematic random sampling method can be caried out.

6　Describe how a stratified random sampling method can be carried out.

Solve.

7　A survey was conducted for a new shopping mall to find out the shopping experience of the customers. Every 10th customer whom walked into the mall was interviewed.

　a　What type of sampling method was used?

　b　Explain whether this sampling method is appropriate.

Extra Practice and Homework
Statistics and Probability

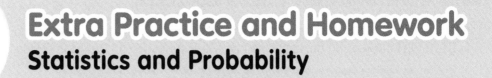

Activity 2   Making Inferences about Populations

Use the dot plot below to answer each question.

1. Emma played a science quiz on the computer. There are 16 rounds for the quiz. The box plot summarizes the points she scored in the game.

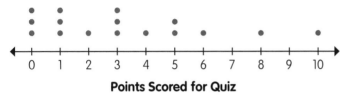

Points Scored for Quiz

a Calculate Q_1, Q_2, and Q_3.

b Calculate the interquartile range.

c Based on the quartiles and interquartile range, what can you infer about her performance for the quiz.

Use the random samples below to answer each question.

2 A survey is carried out to estimate the average number of family members of Grade 7 students. The table below summarizes the results of the survey from 12 randomly selected students.

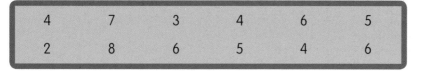

| 4 | 7 | 3 | 4 | 6 | 5 |
| 2 | 8 | 6 | 5 | 4 | 6 |

a Calculate the mean.

b Calculate the mean absolute deviation (MAD).

c From the mean and the MAD, what can you infer about the average size of the family of the students?

Use the random samples below to answer each question.

3 Haley's Math and Science test scores are summarized below.

	Test 1	Test 2	Test 3	Test 4	Test 5
Math Scores	68	76	80	75	81
Science Scores	70	94	58	62	66

 a Calculate the mean scores of both tests.

 b Calculate the MAD of both tests.

c By comparing the mean scores and the MAD of the two tests, what can you infer about Haley's overall performance in the two subjects?

2 A letter is selected from the letters in the word PROBABILITY.
List all the possible types of outcomes.

3 You select a name at random from the list below.

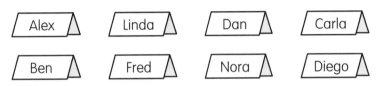

Alex   Linda   Dan   Carla

Ben   Fred   Nora   Diego

a W is the event that the selected name has exactly two different vowels. List the outcomes favorable to event W.

b X is the event that the selected name has 5 letters. List the outcomes favorable to event X.

c Y is the event that the selected name contains the letter r. What outcomes are favorable to event Y?

Use the random samples below to answer each question.

3 Haley's Math and Science test scores are summarized below.

	Test 1	Test 2	Test 3	Test 4	Test 5
Math Scores	68	76	80	75	81
Science Scores	70	94	58	62	66

a Calculate the mean scores of both tests.

b Calculate the MAD of both tests.

c By comparing the mean scores and the MAD of the two tests, what can you infer about Haley's overall performance in the two subjects?

Use the box plots below to answer each question.

  The data of the size of sunflower heads grown in Garden A and Garden B are summarized in two box plots.

Garden A

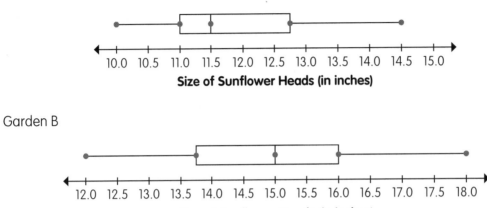

Garden B

Size of Sunflower Heads (in inches)

a Write down Q_1, Q_2, and Q_3 of the size of sunflower heads of the two gardens.

b Calculate the interquartile ranges.

c By comparing the Q_3 of the sunflower heads in Garden A with Q_2 of the sunflower heads in Garden B, write a statement in percent for this comparison.

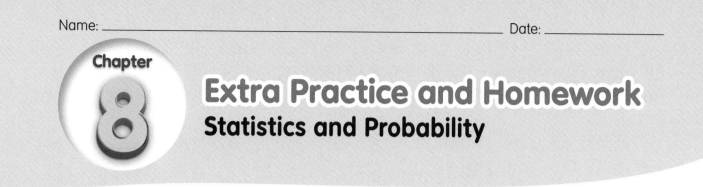

Chapter 8

Extra Practice and Homework
Statistics and Probability

Activity 3   Defining Outcomes, Events, and Sample Space

Solve.

1 Twelve number cards are placed face down. One card is randomly drawn.

a List all the outcomes in the sample space.

b If *A* is the event that the selected card is an even number, what are all the outcomes favorable to event *A*?

c If *B* is the event that the selected card is a prime number, what are all the outcomes favorable to event *B*?

2 A letter is selected from the letters in the word PROBABILITY.
List all the possible types of outcomes.

3 You select a name at random from the list below.

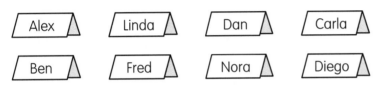

Alex   Linda   Dan   Carla

Ben   Fred   Nora   Diego

a *W* is the event that the selected name has exactly two different vowels. List the outcomes favorable to event *W*.

b *X* is the event that the selected name has 5 letters. List the outcomes favorable to event *X*.

c *Y* is the event that the selected name contains the letter *r*. What outcomes are favorable to event *Y*?

4 A student is selected at random from the tables below.

Name of Student	Wear Glasses? (Yes or No)	Favorite Sport
Ling	No	Tennis
Jake	Yes	Cycling
Rachel	No	Swimming
Luis	No	Tennis
Maria	No	Cycling

Name of Student	Wear Glasses? (Yes or No)	Favorite Sport
Pedro	Yes	Swimming
Matt	Yes	Tennis
Sara	No	Cycling
Roy	Yes	Swimming
Sam	No	Tennis

a *C* is the event that the selected student does **not** wear glasses. List the outcomes favorable to event *C*.

b *D* is the event that the selected student's favorite sport is swimming. List all the possible outcomes of event *D*.

c *E* is the event that the selected student does **not** wear glasses and whose favorite sport is **not** swimming. How many outcomes are favorable to event *E*?

5 A die is rolled and a coin is tossed. One possible outcome is (3, H). (3, H) means the die shows a 3 and the coin shows heads. List all the possible outcomes of the sample space.

6 The 4 numeric tiles [1] [1] [2] [3] are placed face down. You pick 4 tiles to form a 4-digit number. G is the event of forming a 4-digit number greater than 2,000. How many outcomes are favorable to event G?

7 A spinner has 6 values as shown in the diagram.

a List all the outcomes in the sample space.

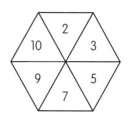

b If event *X* is the event of landing on an odd number, what are the outcomes favorable to event *X*?

c If event *Y* is the event of landing on a prime number, what are the outcomes favorable to event *Y*?

8 A bag contains 3 yellow, 5 blue, and 2 red balls. You pick a ball from the bag. *C* is the event of picking a blue or red ball. How many outcomes are favorable to event *C*?

Chapter 8

Extra Practice and Homework
Statistics and Probability

Activity 4 Finding Probability of Events

Solve.

1️⃣ What is the probability that when you spin the spinner it will land on an odd number?

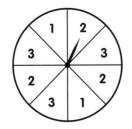

2️⃣ You roll a fair number die. Find the probability of the number die landing on a prime number.

A letter is randomly chosen from the word MATHEMATICS. What is the probability of choosing a vowel?

4 A number is randomly selected from 10 to 20. X is the event of selecting a number divisible by 3. Y is the event of selecting a prime number.

a Draw a Venn diagram to represent the information.

b Are events X and Y mutually exclusive? Explain.

c Find P(X) and P(Y).

5 A dodecahedron number die has 12 faces. Each face is painted with one of the numbers from 1 to 12. Suppose you roll a fair dodecahedron die and record the value on the top face.

a What is the total number of possible outcomes of the sample space?

b Let *A* be the event of selecting an even number. List all the possible outcomes of event *A*.

c Let *B* be the event of selecting a number that is a multiple of 3. Find P(*B*).

d Draw a Venn diagram for the sample space and the two events *A* and *B*. Place all possible outcomes in the Venn diagram.

e From the Venn diagram, tell whether events *A* and *B* are mutually exclusive events? Explain your answer.

f Find the probability of the complement of *B*, P(*B'*).

6 Numbers made up of three digits are formed using the digits 1, 2, and 5 with no repeating digits.

  a List all possible outcomes.

  b Find the probability of randomly forming a number greater than 200.

  c Find the probability of randomly forming a number that is divisible by 5.

7 A deck of picture cards consists of 2 animal cards, 12 flower cards, and 10 blank cards. A student randomly selects a card from the deck.

  a What is the probability that the chosen card is a picture of flowers?

  b What is the probability that the chosen card is blank?

  c What is the probability that the chosen card is **not** blank?

8 In a small town, 55% of the townspeople are local. Of the townspeople, 30% of them speak Spanish. 15% of the townspeople speak Spanish and are local.

a Draw a Venn diagram to represent the information.

b If the town has a population of 3,800, how many local townspeople and townspeople who speak Spanish are there altogather?

c If you randomly select a person in this town, what is the probability that the person is local and does **not** speak Spanish?

9 Sara had 4 red socks, 6 white socks, and 2 pink socks in her drawer. She took a white sock out of the drawer. She wants to randomly pull out another sock from the same drawer.

a What is the probability that Sara pulls out a white sock?

b What is the probability that Sara pulls out a sock that is not white?

c Are the events described in a and b complementary? Explain.

10 1,000 students were surveyed to choose whether they like soft-boiled eggs or scrambled eggs for breakfast. 60% of the students liked soft-boiled eggs and 35% of them liked scrambled eggs. 150 students liked both.

a Draw a Venn diagram to represent the information.

b What percent of the students liked neither soft-boiled eggs nor scrambled eggs?

c What is the probability of choosing a student who only liked scrambled eggs?

11 A factory manufactures 4,800 fluorescent light tubes and light bulbs. The ratio of the number of fluorescent light tubes to the number of light bulbs is 5 : 3. Some of the light tubes and light bulbs are faulty. 1 in every 10 fluorescent light tubes and 1 in every 30 light bulbs are faulty.

a What fraction of the light tubes and bulbs are faulty?

b What is the probability that a randomly selected light bulb is not faulty?

Chapter 8

Extra Practice and Homework
Statistics and Probability

Activity 5 Approximating Probability and Relative Frequency

Solve.

1 A coin is tossed 80 times and lands on heads 36 times.

a Find the relative frequency of the coin landing on heads.

b Find the relative frequency of the coin landing on tails.

c The coin is tossed another 20 times and lands on tails 12 times. Find the relative frequency of the coin landing on tails for 100 tosses.

2 In a day, 160 different flavored yogurt are sold. The table shows the observed frequency for each flavor.

Flavor	Butterscotch	Chocolate	Strawberry	Vanilla
Observed Frequency	30	48	42	40
Relative Frequency				

a Complete the table. Write each relative frequency as a fraction.

b What percent of yogurt sold are chocolate?

c What percent of yogurt cones sold is either strawberry or butterscotch?

3 A number die is tossed 50 times. After each toss, the result is recorded. The table gives the observed frequency for each face value.

Face Value	1	2	3	4	5	6
Observed Frequency	10	6	9	8	10	7

a What is the experimental probability of tossing the die and getting a face value of 5? Give your answer as a percent.

b What is the theoretical probability of tossing the die and getting a face value of 5? Give your answer as a percent.

c The theoretical and the experimental probabilities are not equal. Describe some factors that cause the two probabilities to be different.

d What is the experimental probability of tossing the die and getting an odd face value? Give your answer as a decimal.

e What is the theoretical probability of tossing the die and getting an odd face value? Give your answer as a decimal.

4 In a population study, 20,000 people are classified according to their age. The table shows the observed frequency for each age interval.

Age (A years)	$30 \leq A < 40$	$40 \leq A < 50$	$50 \leq A < 60$	$60 \leq A < 70$
Observed Frequency (10,000)	6	5	5	4
Relative Frequency				

a Complete the table. Write each relative frequency as a percent.

b Find the relative frequency for the people between 40 and 60 years old. Give your answer as a percent.

c If a person is randomly selected, what is the probability that the selected person is older than or is 60 years old but is younger than 70 years old?

d Draw a relative frequency histogram using percent.

5 The histogram shows the Mathematics test scores of 40 students.

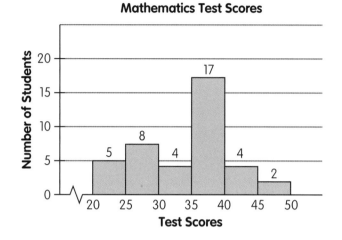

a Complete the table. Give your answer as a decimal.

Test Score (T)	$20 \leq T < 25$	$25 \leq T < 30$	$30 \leq T < 35$	$35 \leq T < 40$	$40 \leq T < 45$	$45 \leq T < 50$
Relative Frequency						

b Find the probability that a randomly selected student has a score between 35 and 45.

c Find the probability that a randomly selected student has a score less than 30.

6 The table shows the relative frequencies of the mass, in grams, of 500 apples.

Mass (M grams)	$334 \leq M < 337$	$337 \leq M < 340$	$340 \leq M < 343$	$343 \leq M < 346$
Relative Frequency	15%	45%	30%	10%

a Draw a relative frequency histogram using percent.

b How many apples have a mass between 337 grams and 343 grams?

c What is the probability that the randomly selected apple has a mass of less than 340 grams? Give your answer as a decimal.

Chapter 8
Extra Practice and Homework
Statistics and Probability

Activity 6   Developing Probability Models

Solve.

1   A fair octahedral number die is a 8-faced number die, which has values from 1 to 8 on its faces. You roll a fair octahedral number die and record the number on the face the number die rests on when it lands.

   a   List all the outcomes in the sample space.

   b   What is the probability of rolling a number less than 5?

   c   Construct a probability model of all possible outcomes.

   d   Present the probability distribution in a bar graph.

   e   If A is the event of rolling a number divisible by 3, find P(A).

2 A spinner with numbers 1, 2, 3, 4, and 5 is used to play a game.
The numbers 1 to 3 appears $\frac{1}{4}$ of the time while the numbers 4 and 5
appears $\frac{1}{8}$ of the time.

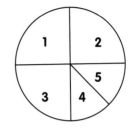

a List all the possible outcomes of the game.

b What is the probability of spinning a 4?

c Construct a probability model for all possible outcomes.

d Is the probability distribution uniform? Explain.

e If E is the event of getting a odd number, find P(E).

A number die with faces numbered 1 to 6 was made incorrectly. When you roll the number die, number 1 appears $\frac{1}{4}$ of the time. Each of the five other numbers has an equal chance of being rolled.

a List all the outcomes in the sample space.

b What is the probability of rolling a 1?

c Construct a probability model of all possible outcomes.

d Present the probability distribution in a bar graph.

e Is the probability distribution uniform? State your reason.

④ The data show the length, in centimeters, of 24 young plants.

| 20.5 | 15.6 | 16.0 | 29.9 | 26.7 | 19.0 | 16.3 | 10.4 | 23.6 | 25.5 | 21.0 | 14.7 |
| 11.8 | 20.8 | 28.1 | 24.3 | 13.0 | 24.9 | 27.4 | 28.7 | 17.0 | 14.1 | 15.8 | 12.8 |

a Complete the following frequency table.

Length of Young Plant (cm)	10–15	15–20	20–25	25–30
Number of Young Plant				

b Construct the probability model.

c Present the probability distribution in a histogram. Is the probability distribution uniform?

d If you randomly pick a plant, what is the probability that the length of the selected plant is at least 20 centimeters?

5 The diagram shows the favorite colors of some students in a class.

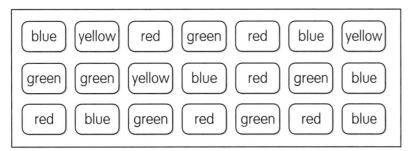

a Complete the following frequency table.

Favorite Color	Red	Yellow	Green	Blue
Frequency				

b Construct the probability model.

c Present the probability distribution in a bar graph. Is the probability distribution uniform?

d If a student is randomly picked from the class, what is the probability that the student does **not** like red?

6 In a game, a student tossed three coins in a row and recorded the sequence of heads or tails that appear. For example, HHT means heads appears first, followed by heads, and lastly tails.

a Give the possible outcomes for the sample space.

b Is this situation an example of a uniform probability distribution? Explain.

c Construct a probability model.

d To win the game, the student had to toss the sequence HTT. What is the probability that the student won the game?

Mathematical Habit 7 Make use of structure

Jake spins spinner *P*, followed by spinner *Q*, and lastly spinner *R*. He notes the results of each spin and adds them together. He says that the probability of getting a sum that is odd is dependent on spinner *P*. Is he correct? Explain your answer.

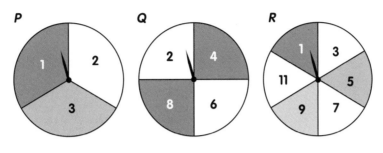

© 2020 Marshall Cavendish Education Pte Ltd

MATH JOURNAL

Mathematical Habit 1 Persevere in solving problems

Hiro tosses 4 coins in a game. He wins if the outcomes of his tosses have more heads. Find the probability that he will win.

2 **Mathematical Habit 1** Persevere in solving problems

A bag contains tiles with the following digits: 2, 3, 5, and 7. Pedro randomly picks a number from the bag. Then, Luis and Rosie each randomly pick a number from the same bag. The three students use their numbers to create a three-digit number. Find the probability that the three-digit number formed is divisible by 5.

A number is divisible by 5 when its digit in the ones place is 0 or 5.

Chapter 9

Extra Practice and Homework
Probability of Compound Events

Activity 1   Compound Events

Determine whether each statement is True or False.

1 Selecting a vowel from the alphabet is a simple event.

2 Getting a two when throwing 2 fair six-sided number dice is a simple event.

3 Getting two tails when tossing 2 coins is a compound event.

4 Selecting a ball labeled 1 from a bag containing 10 balls labeled 1 to 10 is a compound event.

Determine whether each event is a simple or compound event. If it is a compound event, identify the simple events that make up the compound event.

5 Selecting the letter B from the word PROBABILITY

6 Drawing a black pebble followed by a white pebble from a bag containing 5 black pebbles and 5 white pebbles

7 Choosing a day from the month of April

8 Rolling a fair four-sided die twice and obtaining the product of the two numbers

Solve.

9 A spinner with three equal sectors labeled 1 to 3 is spun and a fair six-sided number die is rolled.

    a Draw a possibility diagram to represent the possible outcomes.

    b How many possible outcomes are there?

10 Jenna plays a game involving a regular tetrahedral die and a bag of tiles. The die has four faces labeled A, B,C, and D, and the bag contains 6 titles labeled Q, W, E, R, T, and Y.

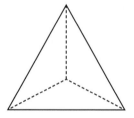

    The die is rolled and the spinner is spun, and the results on each are recorded.

    a Draw a possibility diagram to represent the possible outcomes.

    b How many possible outcomes are there?

11 A bag contains 2 white golf balls and 1 green golf ball. Another bag contains 1 red cube and 2 yellow cubes. Aiden draws a ball from the first bag and a cube from the second bag.

a Use a tree diagram to represent the possible outcomes for drawing a ball and a cube.

b How many possible outcomes are there?

12 A desk drawer contains 2 red, 2 green, and 2 silver paper clips, and 1 black and 2 yellow permanent markers. Brian reaches into the drawer and randomly selects a paper clip and a permanent marker. Use a tree diagram to represent the possible outcomes. Then, tell the number of possible outcomes.

A fair six-sided number die and a fair four-sided number die are tossed at the same time and the sum is recorded.

a Draw a possibility diagram to show the possible outcomes. Then, find the number of favorable outcomes for an even sum.

b Use the possibility diagram to find the number of favorable outcomes for a sum greater than 6.

c Which event is more likely: having a sum that is a prime number or having a sum that is a composite number?

14 Roy randomly selected a digit from his locker combination: 1-2-5-6-3-4 and randomly selected a digit from his computer password: 2-6-1-5-4-3. The product of the numbers were recorded.

a Draw a possibility diagram to show the possible outcomes.

b Use the possibility diagram to find the number of favorable outcomes for a product greater than 20.

c Use the possibility diagram to find the number of favorable outcomes for an odd product.

Chapter 9

Extra Practice and Homework
Probability of Compound Events

Activity 2   Probability of Compound Events

Solve.

1. Bag A contains 1 blue marble and 3 green marbles. Bag B contains 3 blue marbles and 1 green marble. Chase randomly draws a marble from Bag A and another marble from Bag B. Use a possibility diagram to find the probability that the marbles are of different colors.

2. Three colored pens are placed in a backpack, 1 pen with black ink and 2 pens with green ink. First, Peter randomly selects a pen from the backpack. Then, he rolls a fair six-sided number die labeled from 1 to 6. The result recorded is the number facing up. Draw a possibility diagram to represent all the possible outcomes. Then, find the probability of selecting a green pen and getting an even number.

3 Tara rolled a red fair four-sided number die and a yellow fair four-sided number die, each with faces labeled 1 to 4. The results recorded are the numbers facing down. Draw a possibility diagram to represent all the possible outcomes. Then, find the probability that the sum of the numbers is at least 6.

4 A shop sells 3 brands of apple juice, 2 brands of grape juice, and 1 brand of orange juice. The juices are sold in small, medium, and large bottles. A customer randomly selects a bottle of fruit juice. Draw a possibility diagram to represent all the possible outcomes. Then, find the probability that the customer selects a small bottle of apple juice.

5 Ana draws a bead from three numbered beads: 1, 3, and 5. Then, she randomly selects a card from four number cards: 1, 2, 4, and 6. The product of the numbers drawn is recorded.

a Draw a possibility diagram to represent all the possible outcomes.

b Find the probability of getting a product that is greater than or equal to 5, and less than or equal to 10.

6 A letter is randomly chosen from the word BELL, and another letter is chosen randomly from the word BEEP. Draw a tree diagram to represent all the possible outcomes. Then, find the probability that both letters chosen are the same.

7   Bucket A contains a blue hermit crab, a green hermit crab, and a red hermit crab. Bucket B contains a green pebble, a red pebble, and a yellow pebble. Wendy randomly selects a hermit crab from Bucket A and a pebble from Bucket B. Draw a possibility diagram to represent all the possible outomes. Then, find the probability that the crab and the pebble are the same color.

8   Joe randomly draws a disc from a bag containing 2 blue discs and 1 red disc. He then rolls a fair four-sided number die labeled 1, 1, 3, and 4, and records the result. The result recorded is the number facing down. Draw a possibility diagram to represent all the possible outcomes. Then, find the probability of drawing a blue disc and getting a 1.

9 One red tissue and one black tissue are placed in a basket. Randy randomly selects a tissue and notes its color. After replacing the tissue, Randy randomly selects another tissue and notes its color. This process is repeated a third time. Draw a tree diagram to represent all the possible outcomes. Then, find the probability that Randy selected the red tissue more times than the black tissue.

10 Julia writes a letter to each of her three friends. She writes each address on three different envelopes. She then randomly inserts the letters into the three different envelopes. Draw a possibility diagram to represent all the possible outcomes. Then, find the probability that all of the letters correspond to the correct envelope.

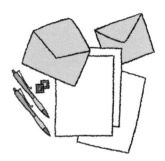

Chapter

9

Extra Practice and Homework
Probability of Compound Events

Activity 3   Independent Events

Draw a tree diagram to represent each situation.

 Popping a balloon randomly from a centerpiece consisting of 1 black balloon and 1 white balloon, followed by tossing a fair six-sided number die

2 Randomly selecting a marble, replacing it, and randomly selecting a marble again from a bag containing 1 black marble, 1 green marble, and 1 red marble

3 Drawing a bead randomly from a bag containing 1 green bead, 1 red bead, 1 white bead, and 1 black bead, followed by tossing a fair coin

4 Randomly drawing three tokens, and replacing each one before the next draw, from a bag containing one $2 token and one $5 token

5 Recording the weather outcome for each day as either rain or shine for four consecutive days, assuming that each outcome is equally likely

6 Randomly choosing a mode of transportation from bus, car, or train, on Saturday and Sunday, assuming all are equally likely

Solve.

7 A game is played using a fair coin and a fair six-sided number die. An outcome of heads on the coin and 5 or 6 on the die wins the game.

a Draw a tree diagram to represent the possible outcomes of this game.

b Find the probability of winning the game in one try.

c Find the probability of losing the game in one try.

8 There are 2 green party hats and 3 red party hats on a table. Ken randomly selects a party hat from the table. He tries the hat on, and then places it back on the table. He randomly selects another party hat.

a Draw a tree diagram to represent the possible outcomes.

b Find the probability that Ken selects 2 red party hats.

c Find the probability that Ken selects a red party hat after he first selects a green party hat.

9 Amy has 1 green bead, 2 red beads, and 3 yellow beads in her bag. She randomly selects a bead from her bag, and replaces it before she randomly selects again.

a Draw a tree diagram to represent the possible outcomes.

b Find the probability that she selects 2 red beads.

c Find the probability that she selects 2 yellow beads.

d Find the probability she selects 2 beads of different colors.

10 A box contains 2 blue cards, 3 red cards, and 5 yellow cards. Tim randomly selects a card from the box, and replaces it before he randomly selects again.

   a Draw a tree diagram to represent the possible outcomes.

   b Find the probability that he selects 2 red cards.

   c Find the probability that he selects a blue card, followed by a yellow card.

   d Find the probability that he selects a yellow card, followed by a red card.

11 Jamie has two fair six-sided number dice, one white and one red. He tosses the red die followed by the white die.

a Find the probability of tossing an odd number on both dice.

b Find the probability of tossing an odd number on the red die and an even number on the white die.

c Find the probability of tossing a number greater than 4 on both dice.

12 The probability of Mandy getting to school on time on any given day is $\frac{9}{10}$. What is the probability of Mandy getting to school late on at least one of any two consecutive days?

13 A spinner has a 60° green sector, a 120° blue sector, and a 180° red sector. Harry spins the spinner twice.

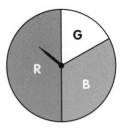

a Find the probability that the spinner points to the same color on both spins.

b Find the probability that the spinner points to the blue sector at least once.

14 A game is designed so that a player wins when the game piece lands on or passes the box W. The game piece starts on box S. A fair six-sided number die is tossed. If the number tossed is 1 or 2, the game piece stays put. If the number tossed is 3 or 4, the game piece moves one box to the right. If the number tossed is 5 or 6, the game piece moves two boxes to the right.

S		W	

a Find the probability that a player will win after tossing the die once.

b Find the probability that a player will win after tossing the die twice.

15 A target board consists of two concentric circles with radii of 3 inches and 6 inches. Claire thinks that the probability of tossing a coin and it landing on the shaded part is $\frac{1}{2}$ since $OA = AB = 3$ inches. Do you agree with her? Explain.

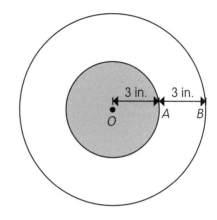

Chapter 9

Extra Practice and Homework
Probability of Compound Events

Activity 4　Dependent Events

Determine whether each pair of events is dependent or independent.

1　Drawing 2 green marbles randomly, one at a time without replacement, from a bag containing 10 blue marbles and 10 green marbles

2　Tossing a fair six-sided number die twice

3　Selecting 2 balloons at random from a bouquet of ordinary colored balloons

4　Tossing a coin three times

Draw a tree diagram for each situation.

5　Two beads are drawn at random, one at a time without replacement, from a bag of 2 blue beads and 3 red beads.

6　The probability that it rains on a particular day is $\frac{1}{4}$. If it rains, then the probability that it rains the next day is $\frac{1}{3}$. If it does not rain, then the probability that it does not rain the next day is $\frac{3}{5}$.

Solve.

7 Owen has a bag of 10 colored balls: 3 green, 3 red, and the rest yellow. He randomly draws two balls, one at a time without replacement.

   a Find the probability of drawing 2 red balls.

   b Find the probability of drawing at least 1 yellow ball.

8 A bag contains 2 black socks, 4 red socks, and 6 white socks. Linda randomly picks two socks from the bag, one at a time without replacement.

   a Find the probability that the socks are of the same color.

   b Find the probability that the socks are of different colors.

There are 12 picture cards, 20 red cards, and 20 black cards in a deck. Timothy and Jane each randomly pick a card from the deck. Timothy picks a card first before Jane picks.

a Find the probability that Timothy and Jane both pick picture cards.

b Find the probability that Timothy picks a red card and Jane a black card, or vice versa.

10 The probability diagram shows the probability of rain on two consecutive days. The probability of rain on a particular day is denoted by x.

a If $x = \frac{1}{3}$, what are the values of y and z? Find the probability that it rains on exactly one of the two days.

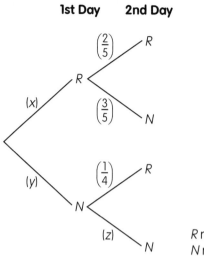

1st Day   2nd Day

R represents rain
N represents no rain

b If the probability of it raining on both days is $\frac{3}{10}$, find the value of x and of y.

11 A fruit basket contains 3 apples, 4 oranges, and 5 pears. Peter and Pedro each randomly select a fruit from the basket.

   a Draw a tree diagram to represent the outcomes.

   b Find the probability that Peter selects an apple and Pedro selects a pear.

   c Find the probability that an orange is selected by either Peter or Pedro.

12 Among a group of 15 students, 4 have blue eyes, 5 have green eyes, and the rest have brown eyes. Two of the students are randomly selected, one after another.

a Draw a tree diagram to represent the possible outcomes.

b What is the probability that the first student selected has brown eyes?

c What is the probability that the first student selected has blue eyes, followed by a student with green eyes?

13 A bag contains 12 nuts: *x* are almonds and the rest are walnuts. Maria randomly selects and eats a nut, followed by Nora.

a If the probability that Maria eats an almond is $\frac{1}{3}$, find the value of *x*.

b Draw a tree diagram to show the possible outcomes.

c What is the probability that Maria and Nora both eat the same type of nut?

14 Alex and Ben play against each other in a game. The probability that Alex wins a particular game is 0.6. If he wins, the probability that he wins the next game is x. If he loses, the probability that he wins the next game is 0.5.

a If the probability that Alex wins both games is 0.42, what is the value of x?

b Draw a tree diagram to show the possible outcomes.

c What is the probability that Ben wins both games?

d What is the probability that Ben wins at least one of the games?

Name: _____ Date: _____

Mathematical Habit 3 Construct viable arguments

David and Betty are discussing whether throwing the same die twice is a dependent or independent event. David thinks it is a dependent event because the same die is being used twice. Betty thinks it is an independent event because the result of the second throw is independent of the first throw. Who is correct? Explain.

1 **Mathematical Habit 1** Persevere in solving problems

In tennis, a player is allowed a second serve if their first serve is a fault. Diego has a first serve which wins him 75% of the points if it is not a fault, but he only succeeds in getting it in play one out of four times. His second serve is not a fault three out of five times, but he only wins 55% of the subsequent points. What percentage of points can Diego expect to win when he is serving?

2 **Mathematical Habit 8** Look for patterns

An integer between one and one million inclusive is randomly chosen. Find the probability that it is not a perfect square.